I0393176

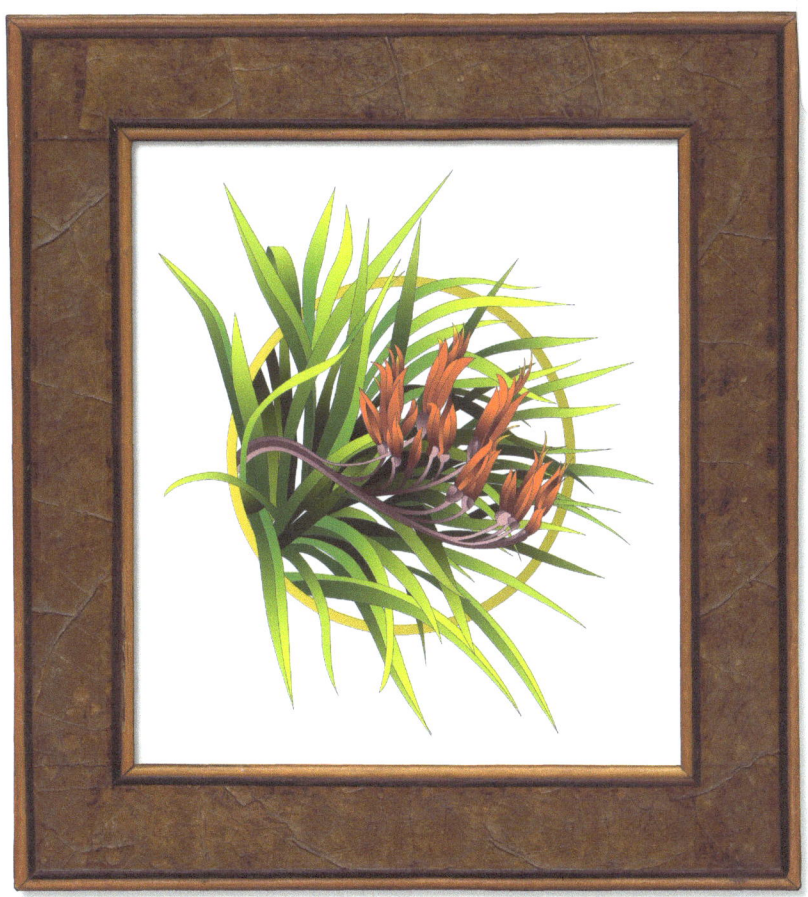

Colour your way to calm.

The health benefits of creativity are scientifically proven.
Making art is good for you!

Take time out to colour these beautiful images and you will be amazed
at the level of relaxation and calm you will achieve.

In this, my second colouring book, I have taken
inspiration from nature, selecting 20 of the New Zealand's flora and fauna.
Tap into your animal instincts and go wild with colour.

Two blank pages have been placed between each set of images to ensure
there is no bleed-through if using marker pens. Enjoy!

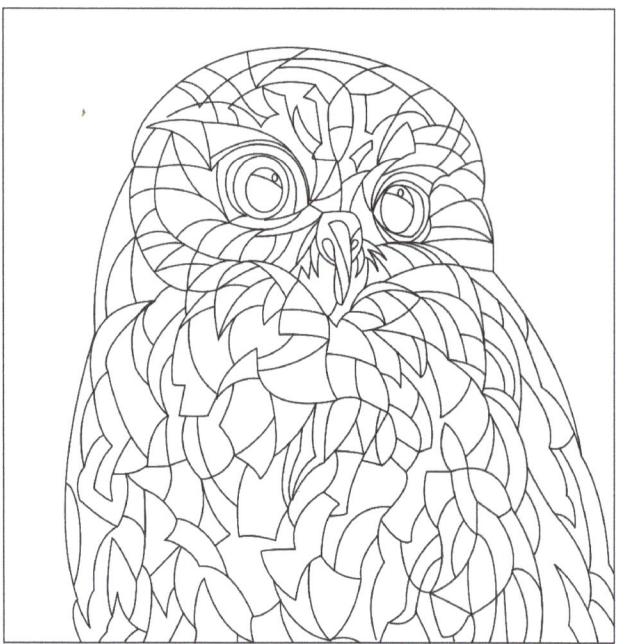

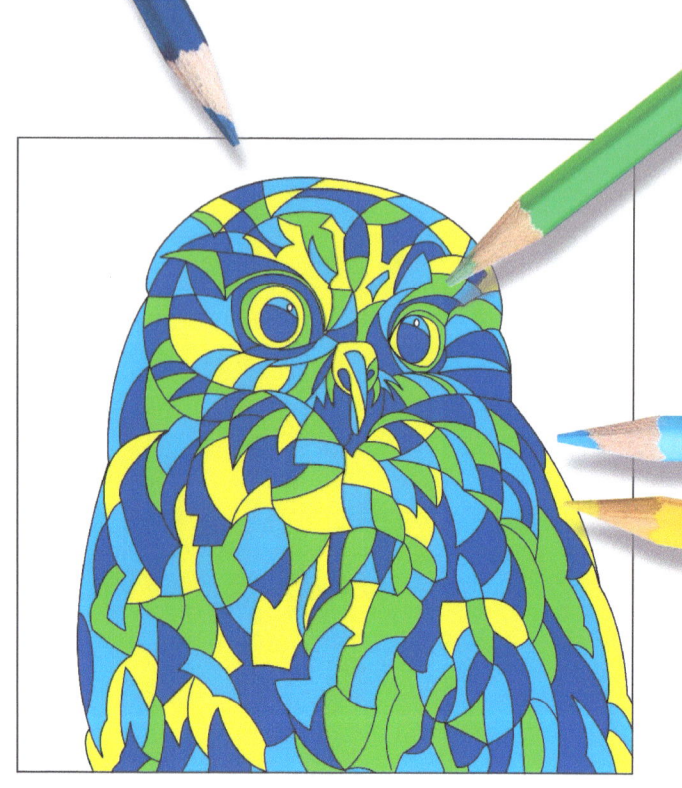

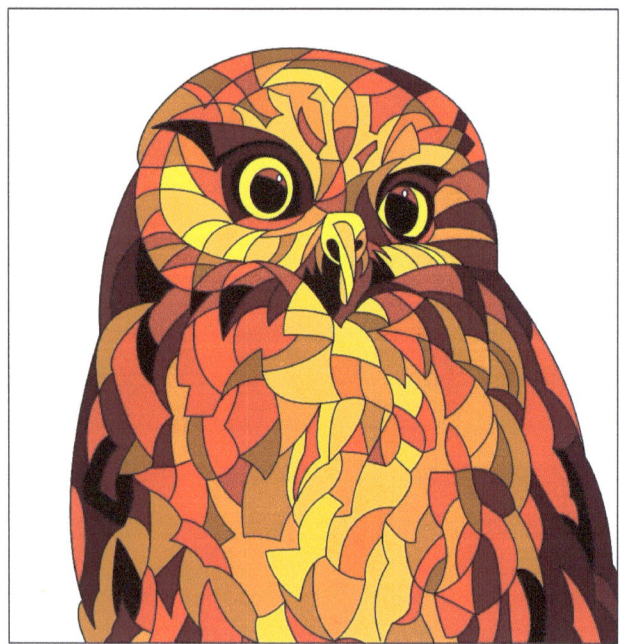

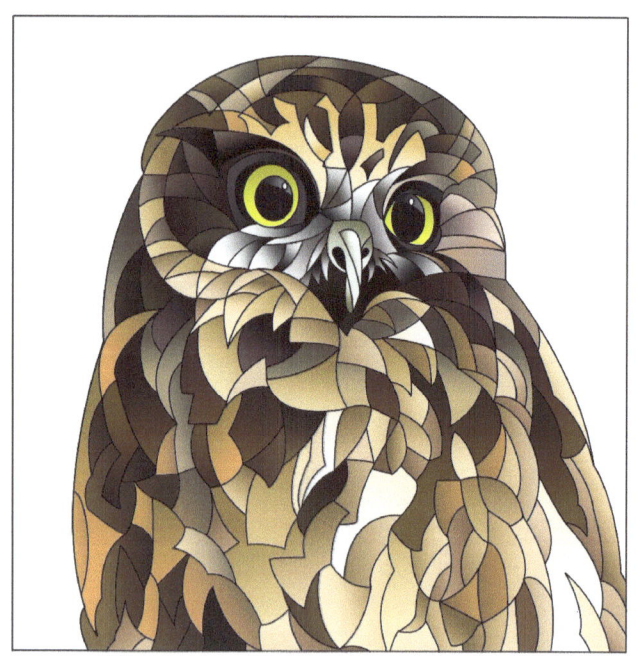

RURU (Morepork)

The morepork is a small brown owl found throughout New Zealand. Known for its distinctive "more-pork" call, it can be found in most habitats with trees, including farmland, alpine grasslands and well-vegetated suburban areas. Typically at night, the morepork hunts a variety of suitably sized prey, including insects, small mammals and birds.

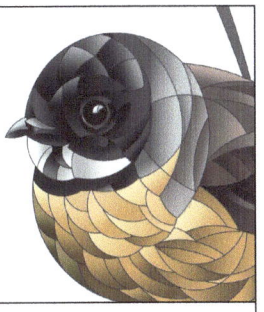

PĪWAKAWAKA (Fantail)

With its distinctive fanned tail, loud song, and famously friendly nature, the fantail is one of New Zealand's best known birds. Eating mainly small insects, the fantail frequents a wide variety of habitats, including both native and exotic forest as well as orchards, scrubland, and well-treed suburban parks and gardens.

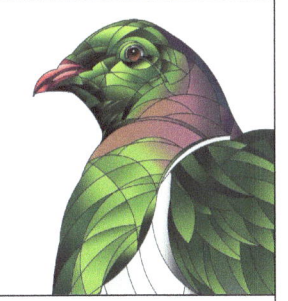

KERERŪ (New Zealand pigeon)

Commonly called a wood pigeon, the large and distinctively-coloured kereru is widespread in New Zealand and can be found in native forests and scrub, as well as rural and urban gardens and parks. Kereru primarily eat fruits from native trees, and play an important role in dispersing native seeds.

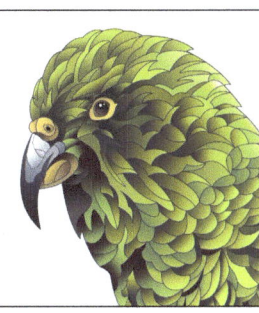

KEA

The only true alpine parrot in the world, the kea is notorious for its curious and intelligent nature. Found in the river valleys, coastal forests, and alpine regions of the South Island, the kea's omnivorous diet consists of several plants, insects, birds and mammals, including rabbits.

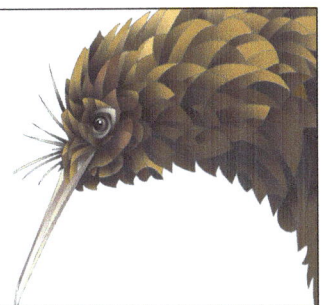

KIWI

The kiwi is a small, shy flightless bird with a highly developed sense of smell. A national symbol of New Zealand, there are five species of kiwi found throughout the country, all of which are gravely threatened by deforestation and introduced predators like stoats, dogs and ferrets.

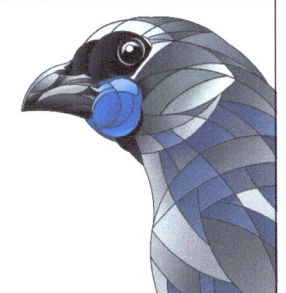

KŌKAKO

With its beautiful, organ-like song that can carry for several kilometres, the kokako is a symbol of ancient Aotearoa New Zealand and a feature of Maori mythology. Though there are two species, the South Island kokako is presumed extinct. The North Island kokako has persisted in small populations through careful pest management.

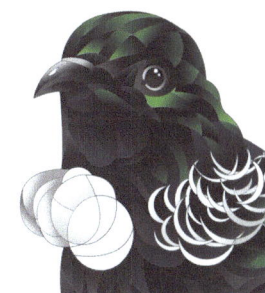

TŪĪ

Tui feathers have a multicoloured iridescent sheen with a distinctive white throat tuft. Found throughout the North Island, the west and south coasts of the South Island, as well as islands off the mainland, they are known for their noisy and complicated repertoire of vocalisations, which are often unique to each individual bird.

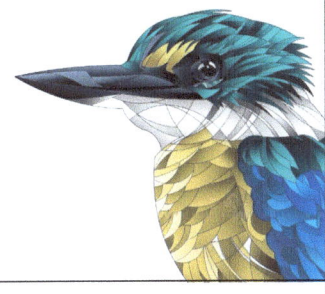

KŌTARE (Kingfisher)

Known to Maori as the kotare, the sacred kingfisher is well-known in New Zealand, distinguished by its habit of perching in elevated observation posts and patiently waiting for prey to appear, at which point it swoops down to grab the unsuspecting insect, lizard, small bird or mammal.

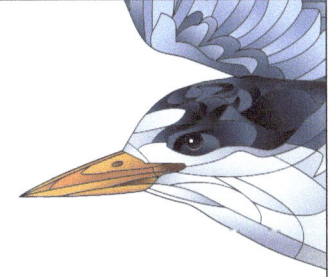

TARA-ITI (Fairy tern)

New Zealand's most threatened endemic bird, the dainty tara-iti is found only sparsely in the North Island, from Auckland to Whangarei. With a diet consisting of small coastal and estuarine fish and shrimps, the bird's tiny population is hugely threatened by urban development, human disturbance and introduced predators.

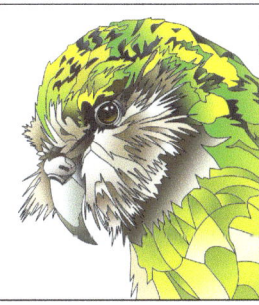

KĀKĀPŌ

The kakapo is unique among parrots, being nocturnal, flightless, herbivorous, and uncommonly large. Once prevalent throughout New Zealand, predation by introduced mammals has since brought the species close to extinction. Now limited to predator-free islands off the mainland of New Zealand, population numbers are slowly increasing through intensive intervention efforts.

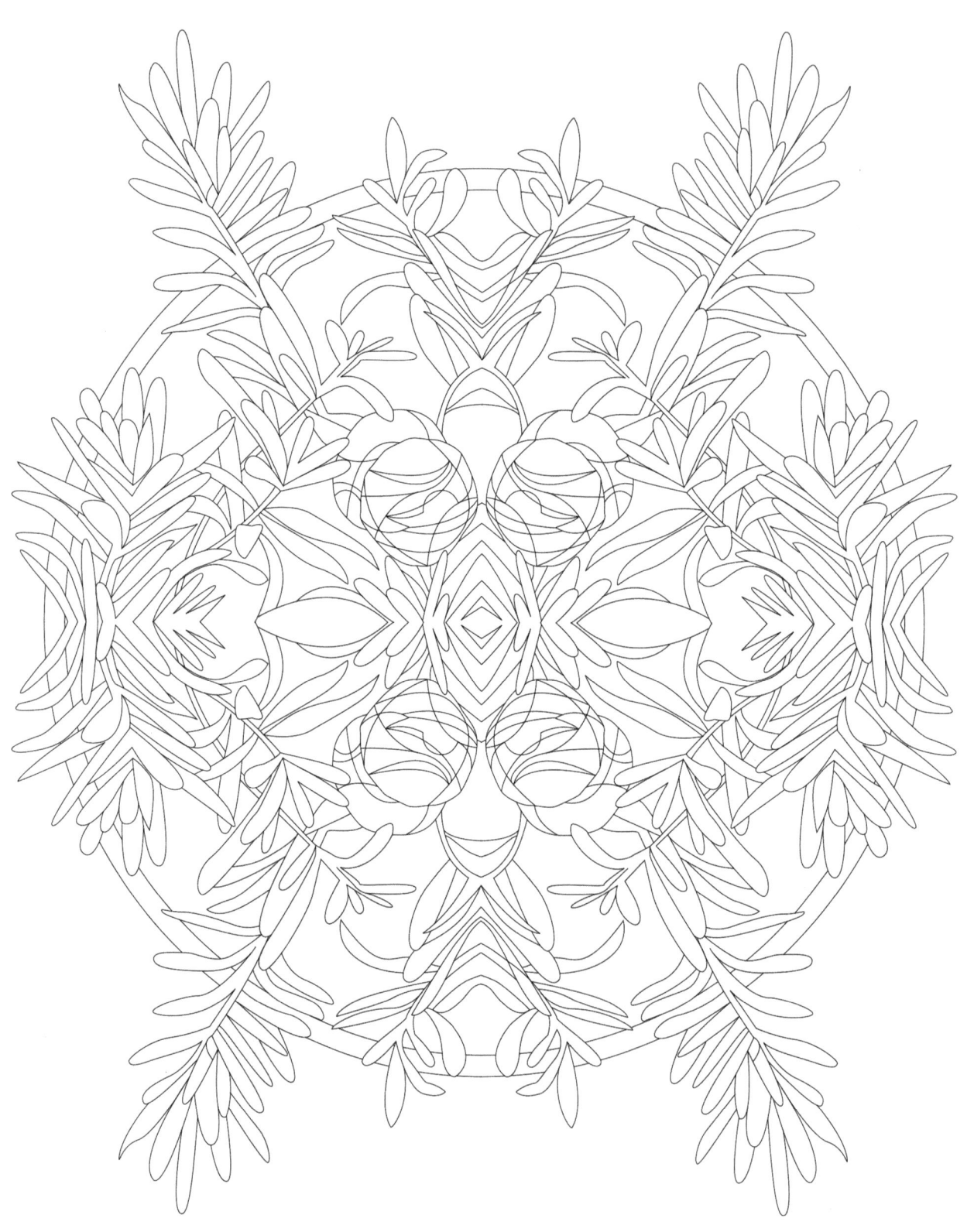

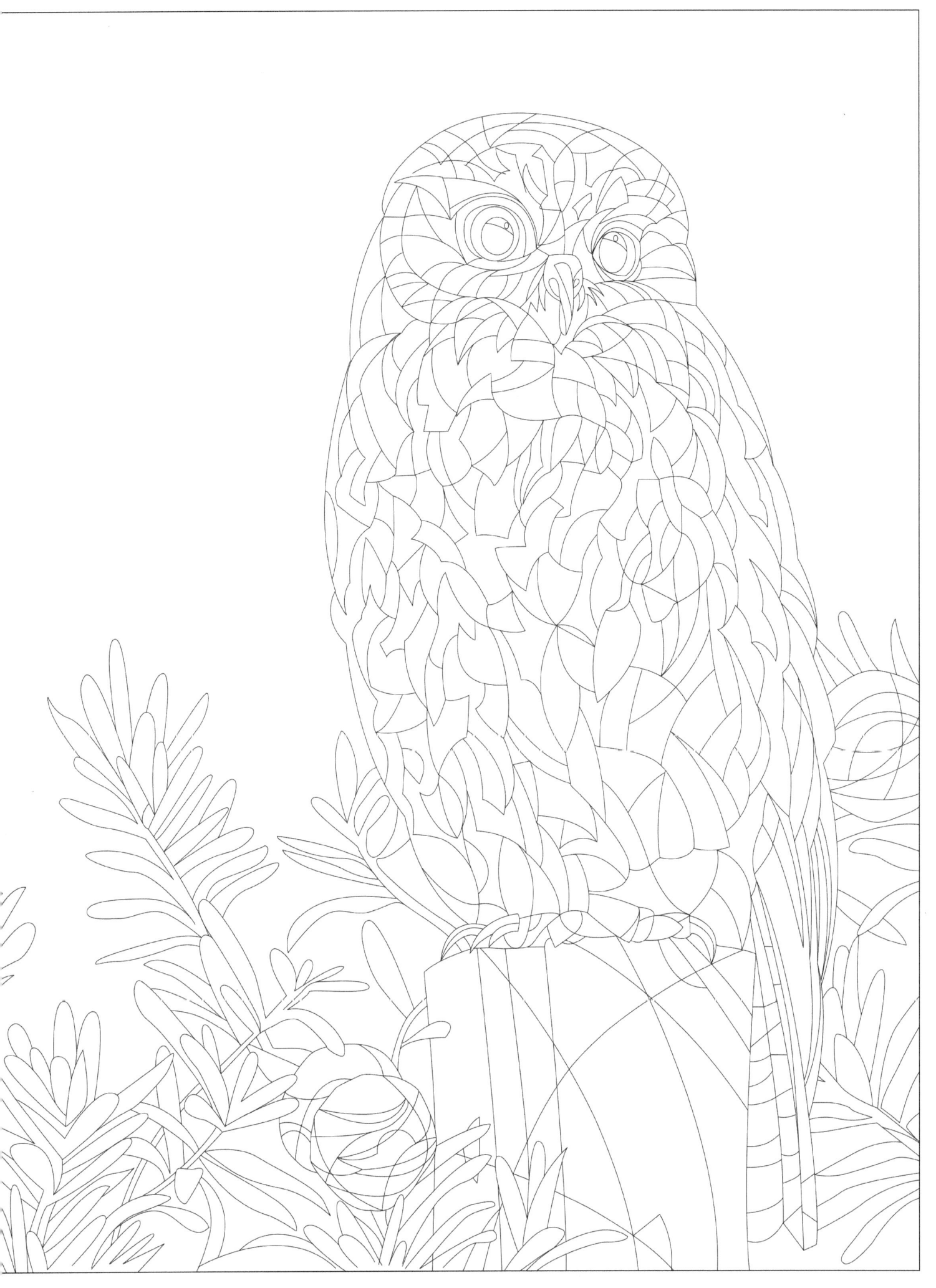

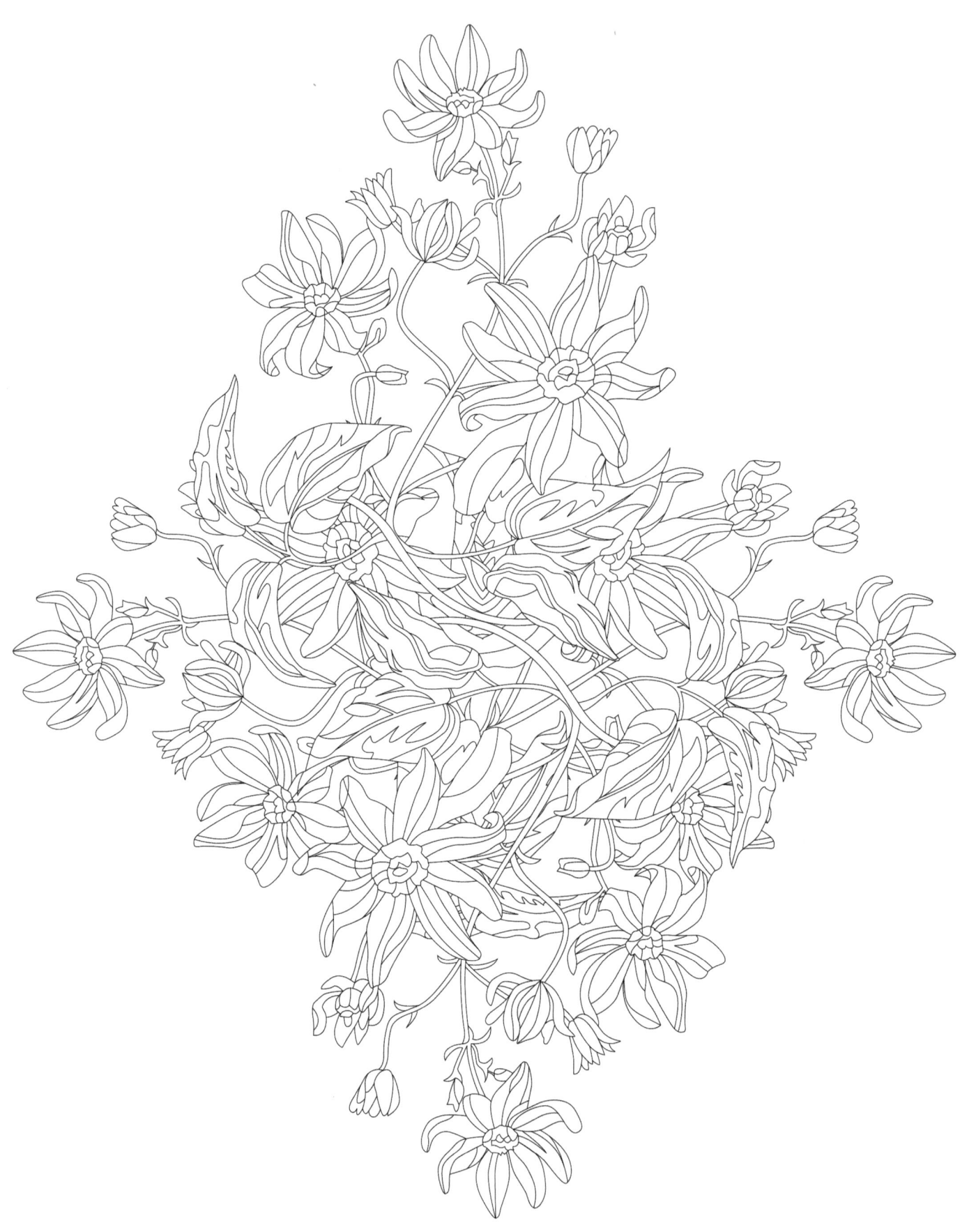

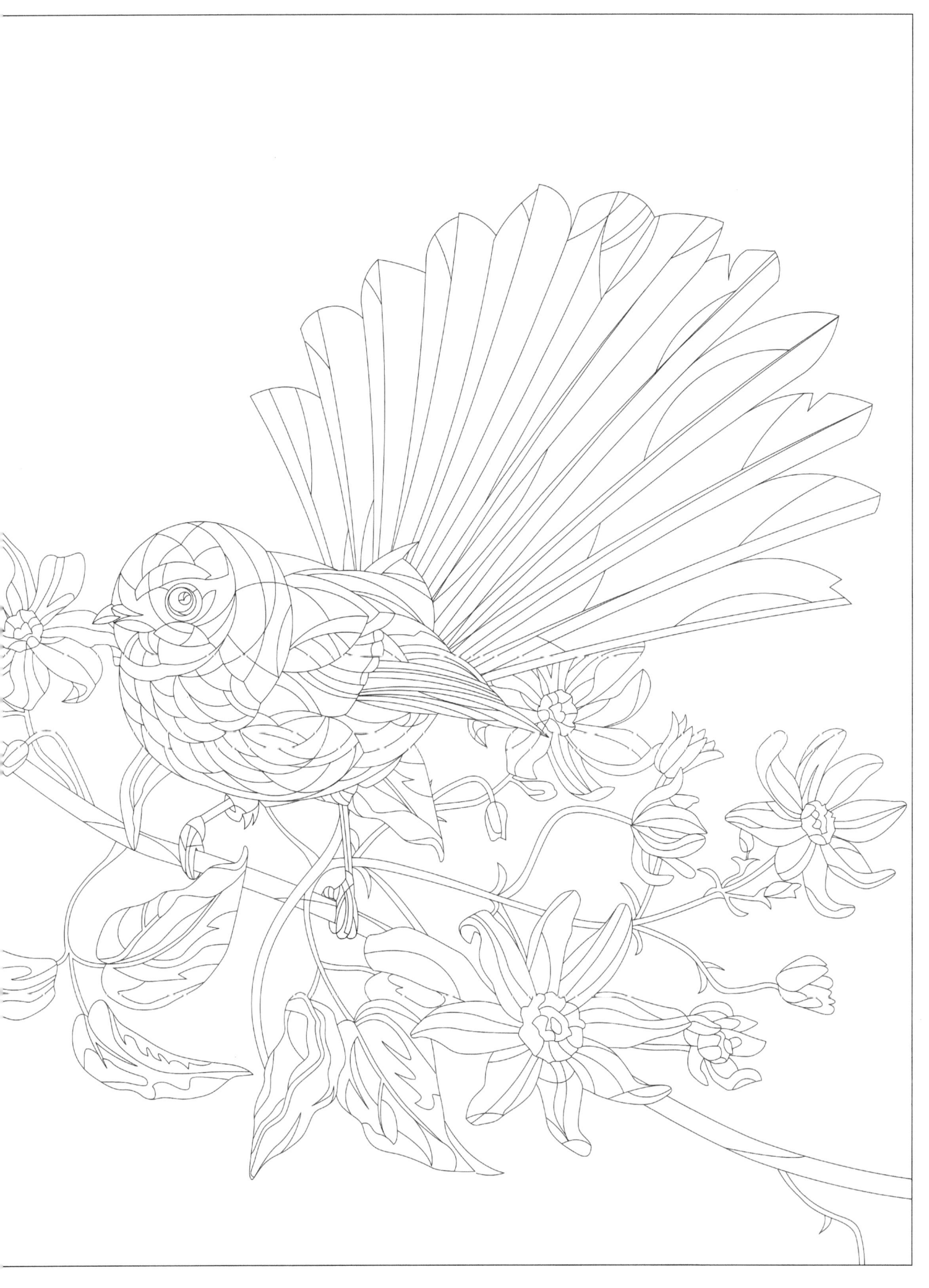

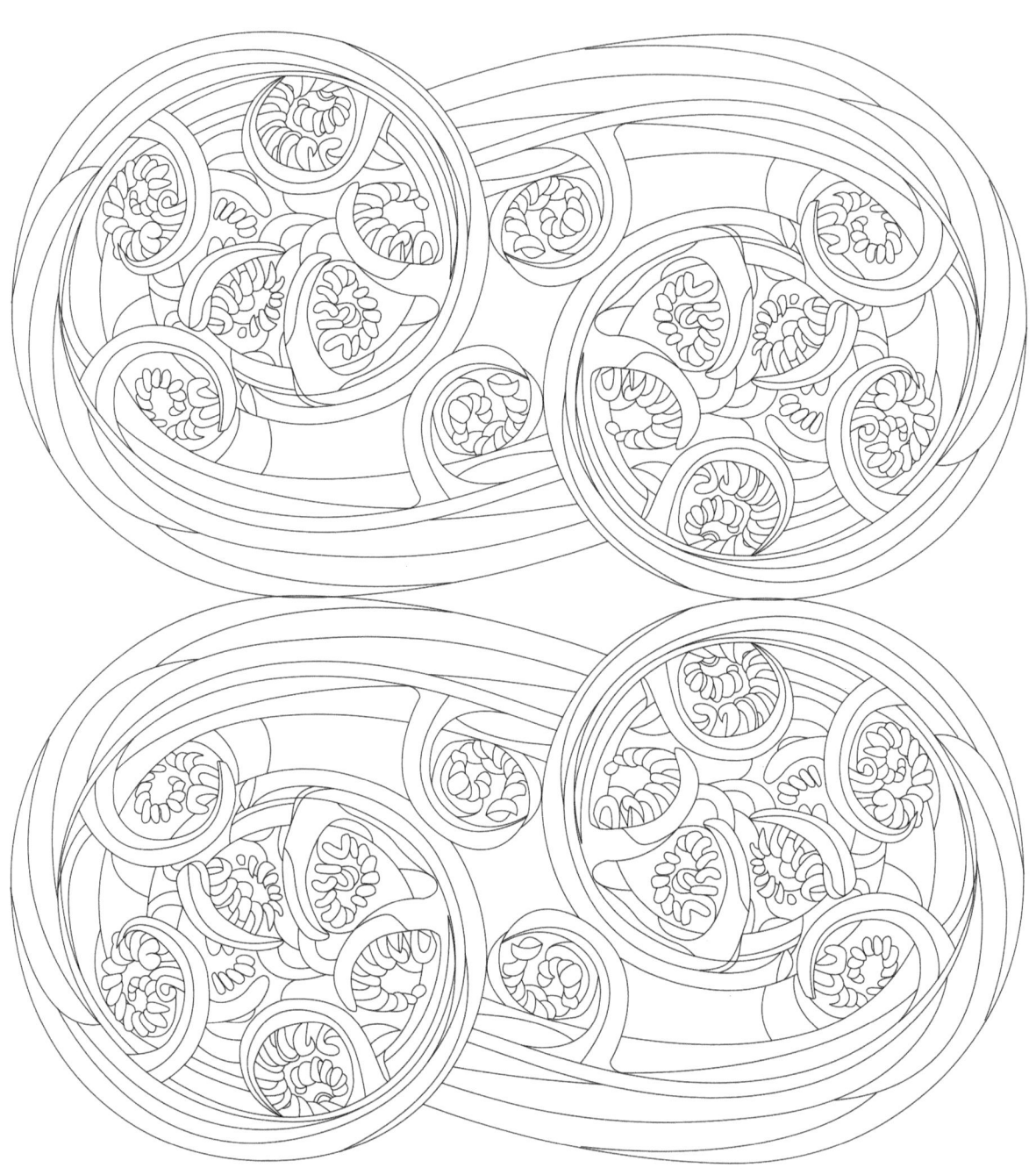

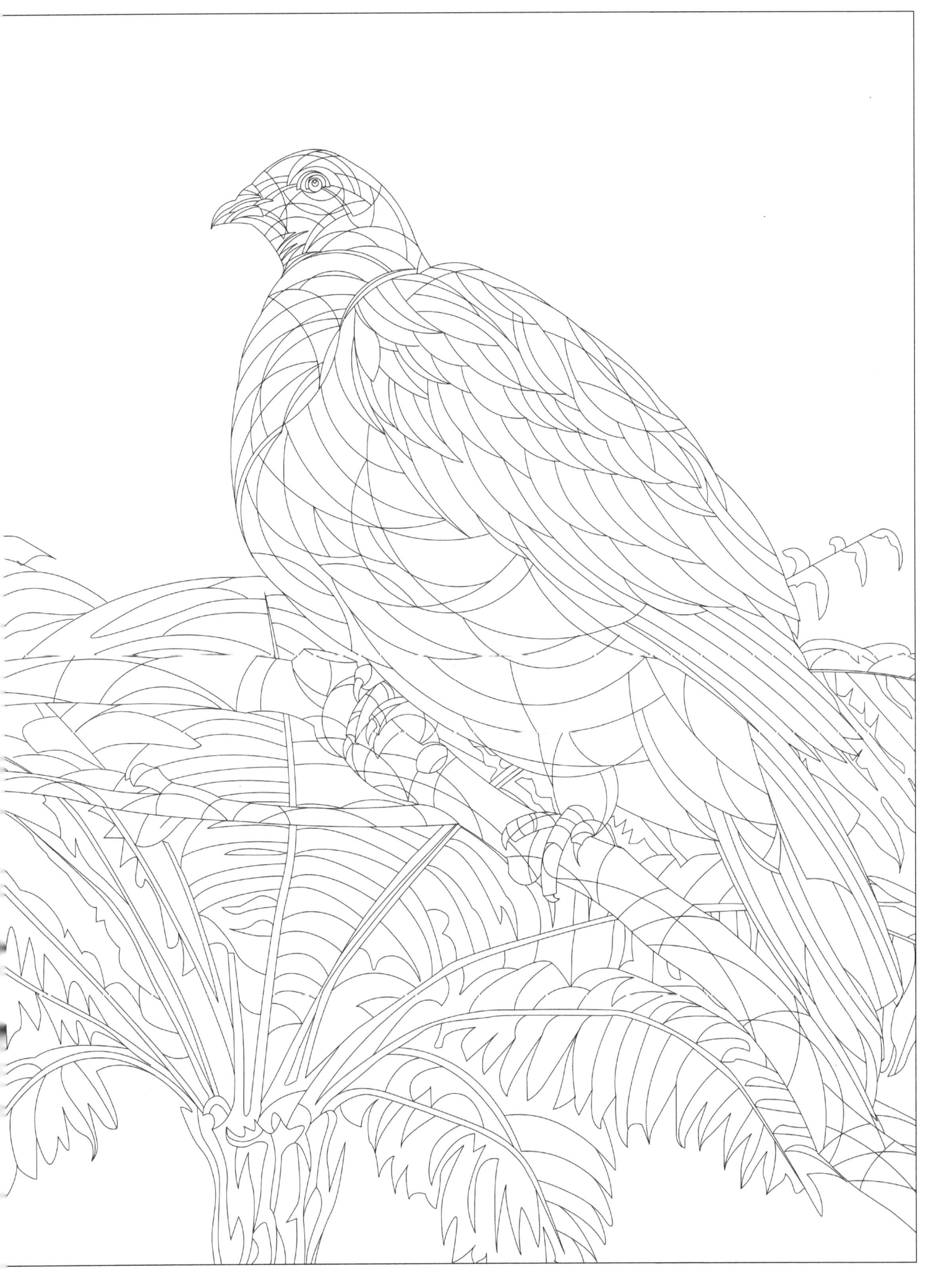

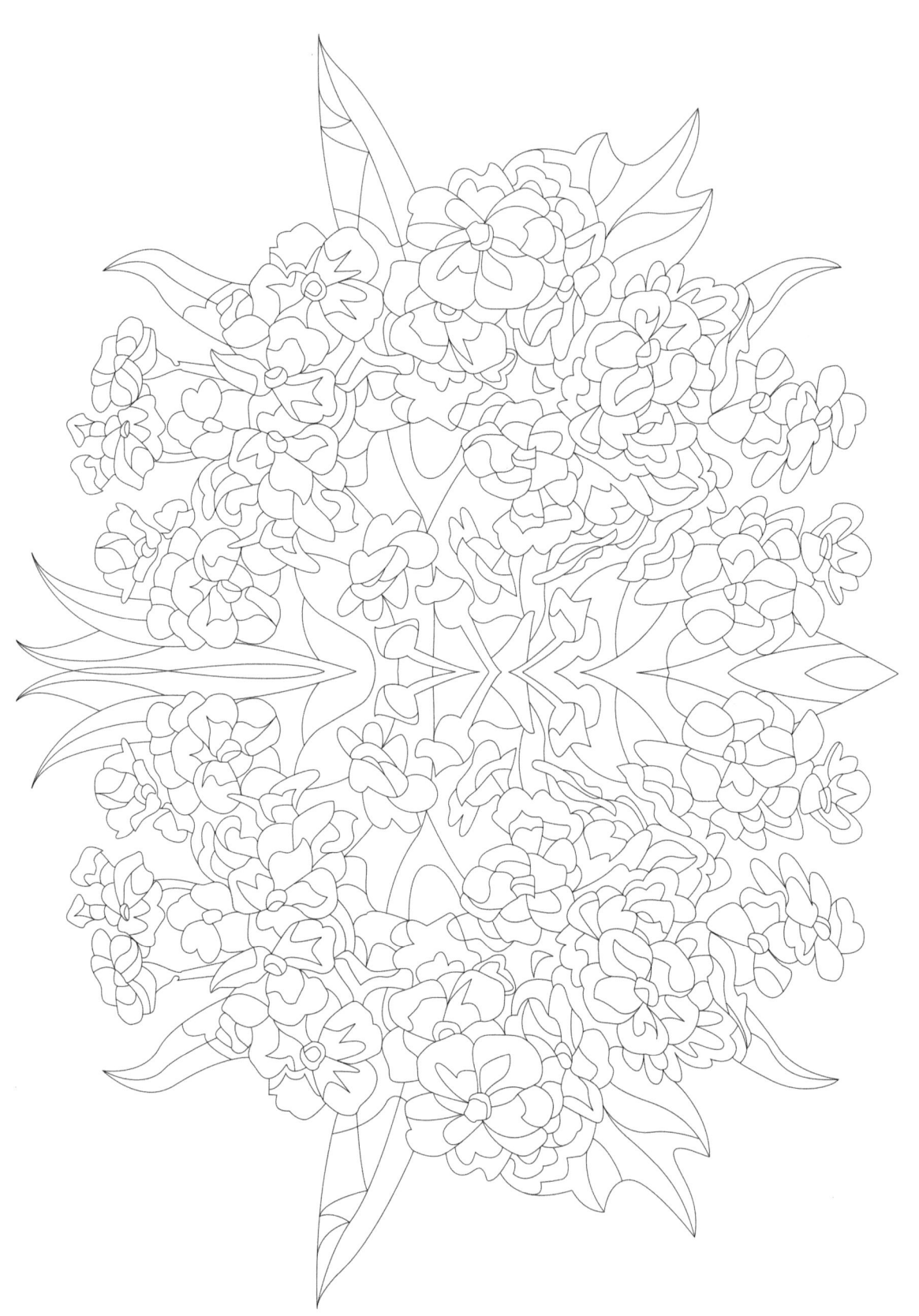

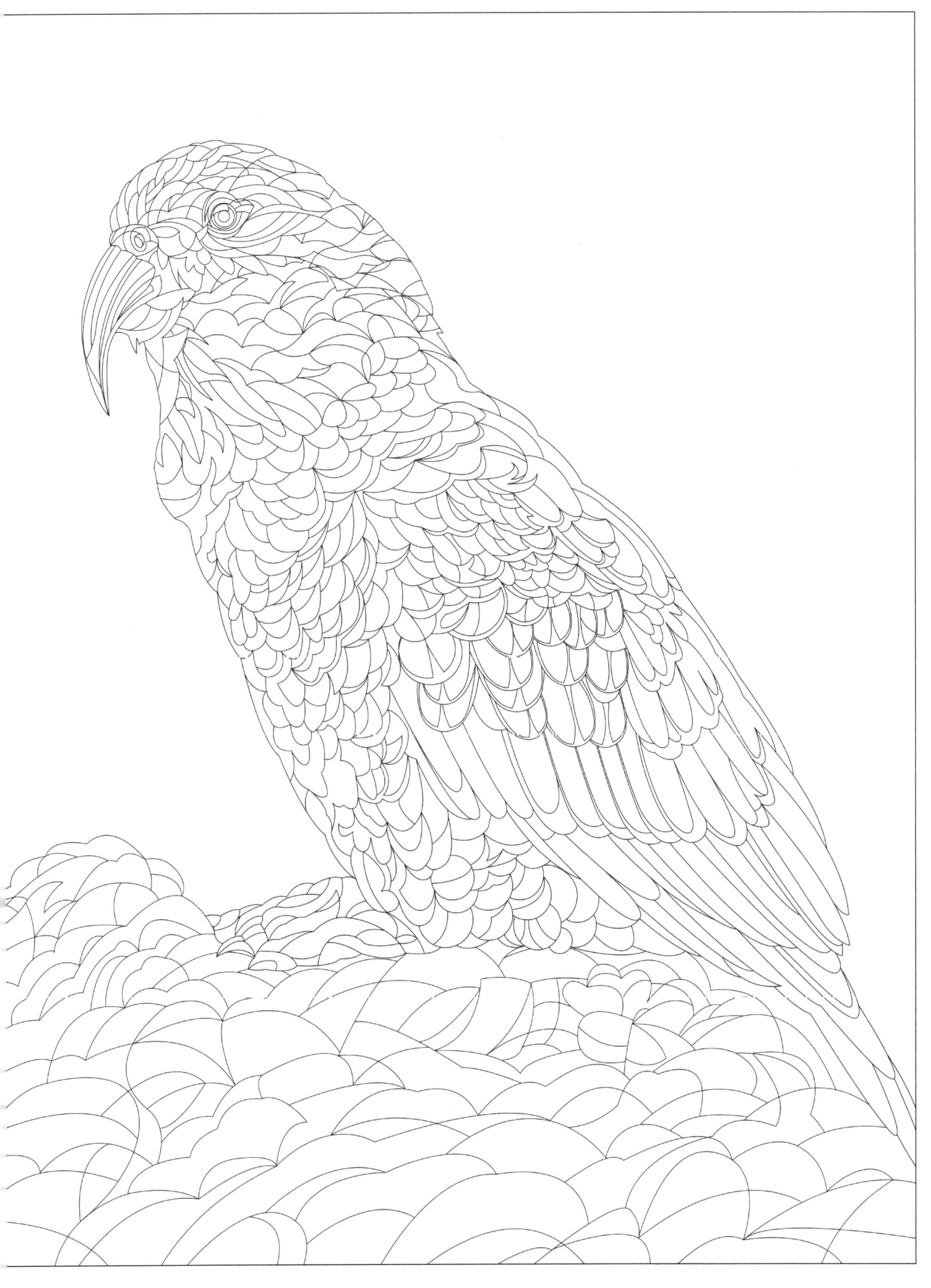

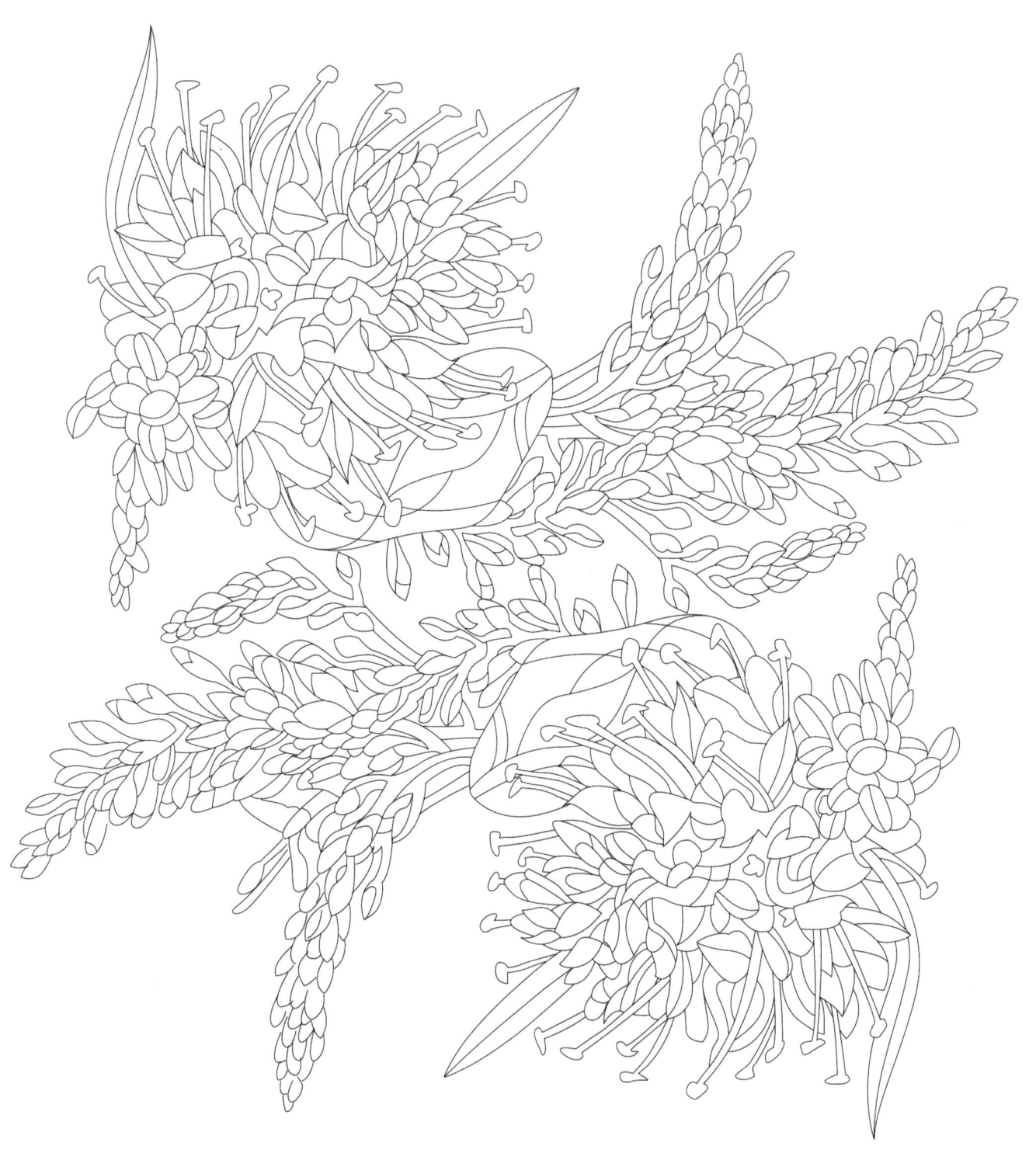

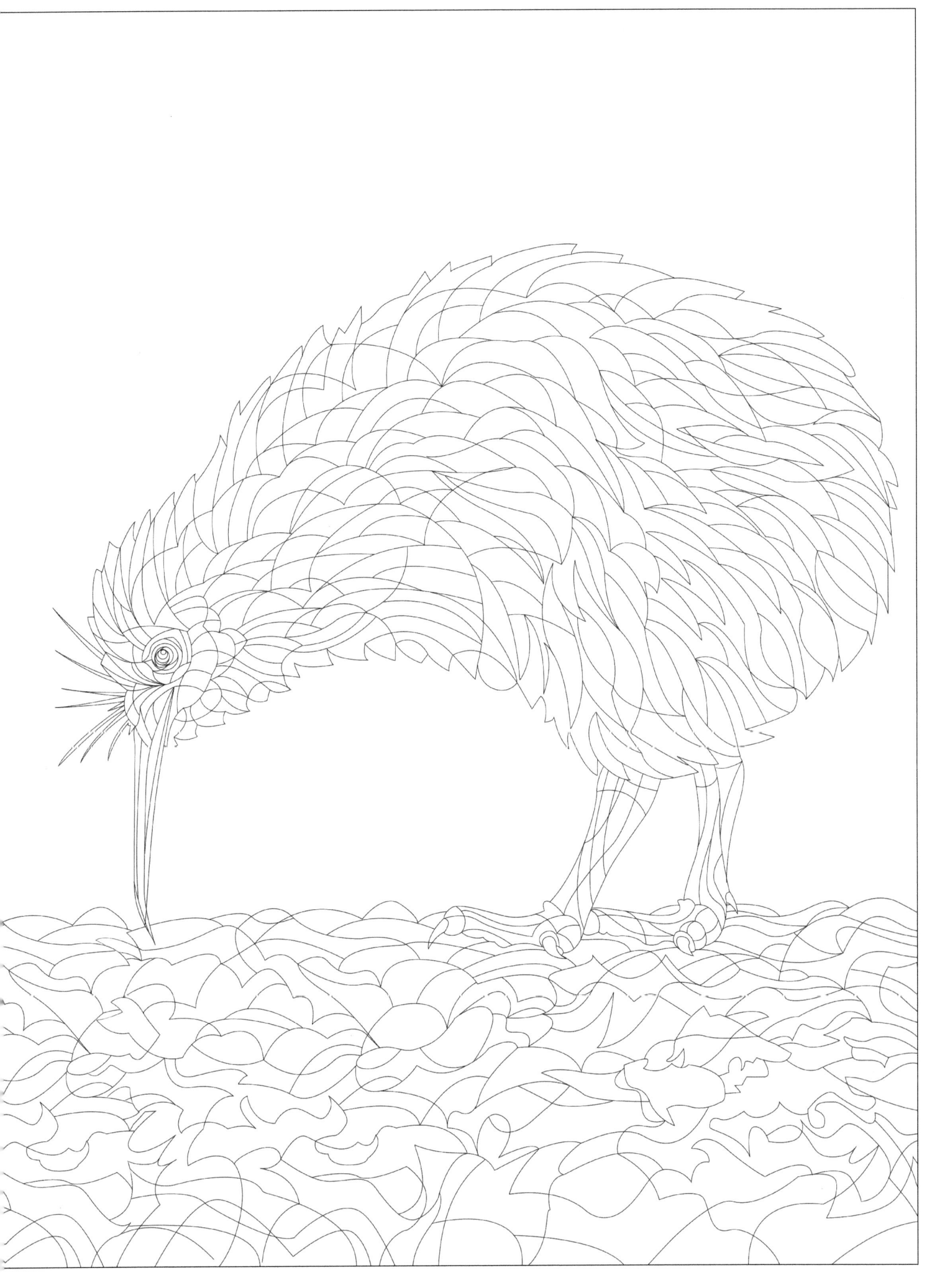

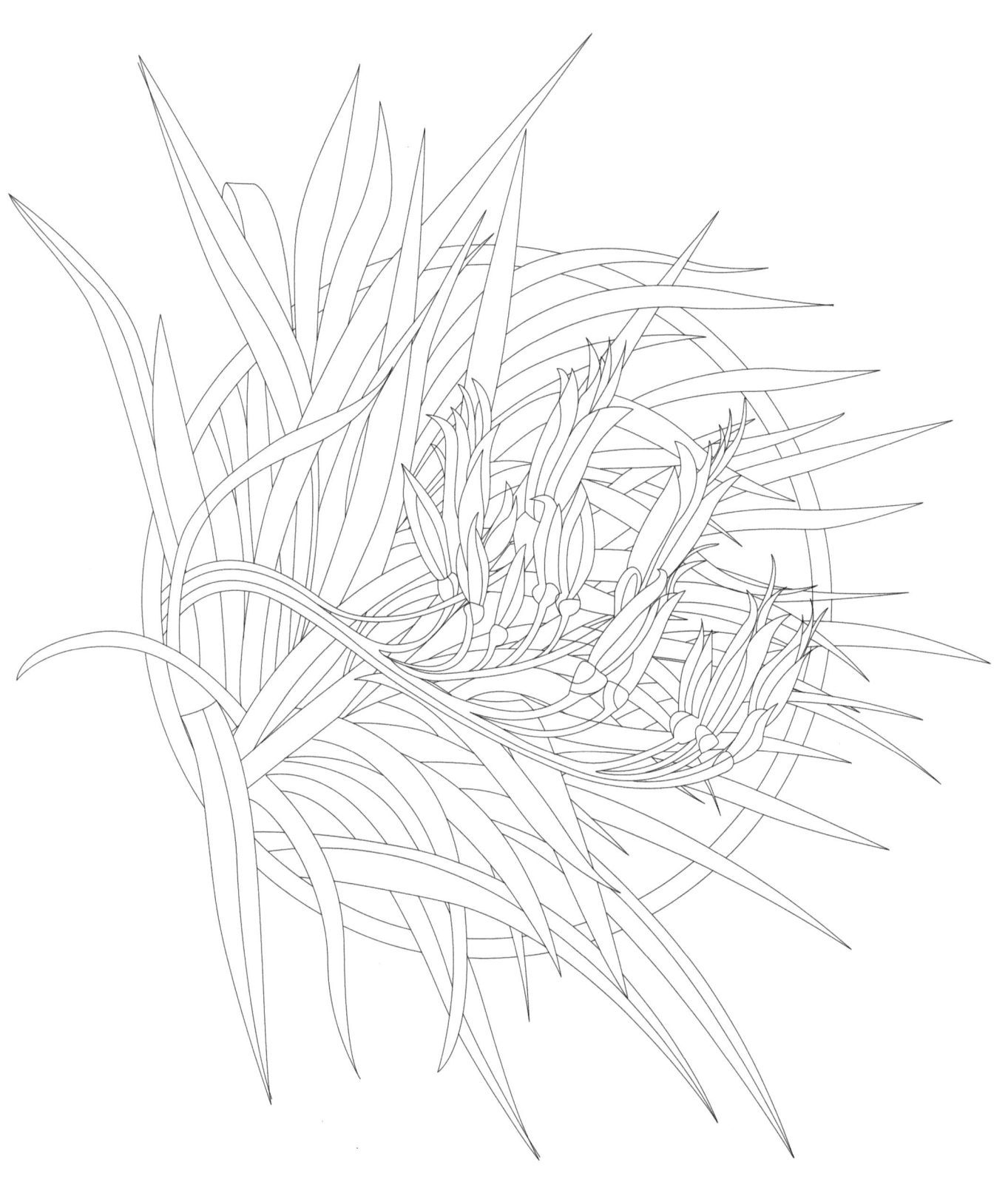

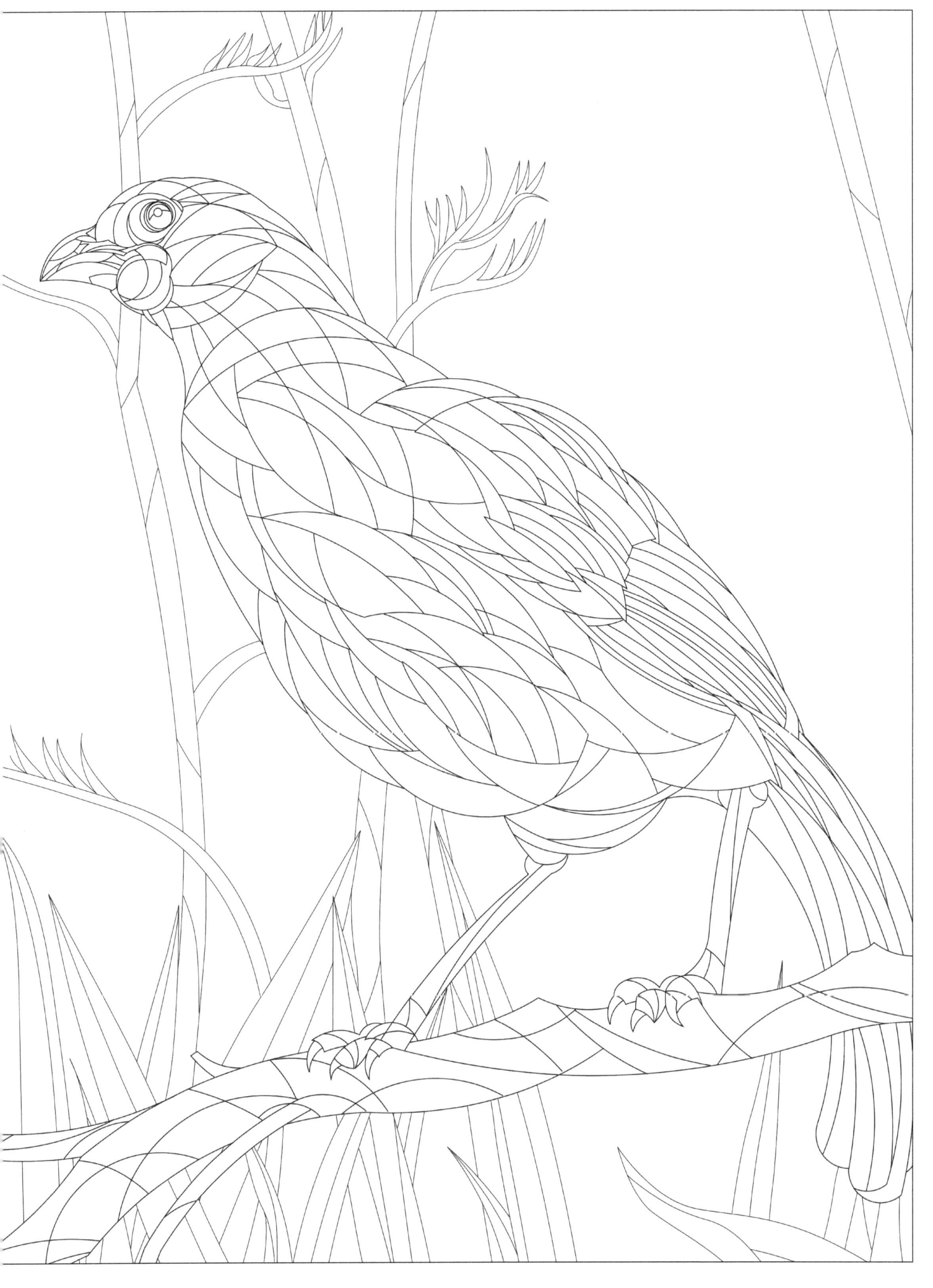

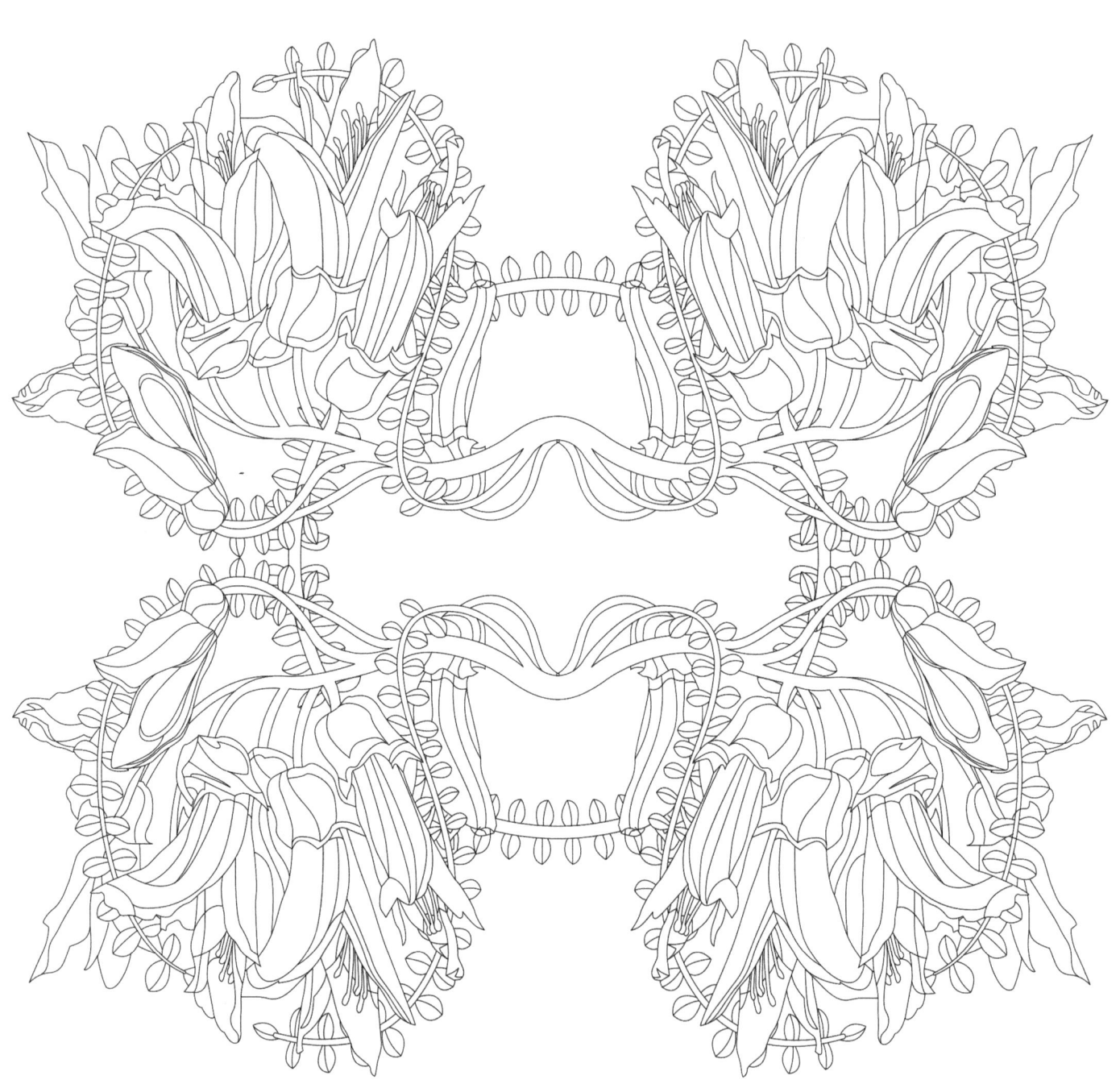

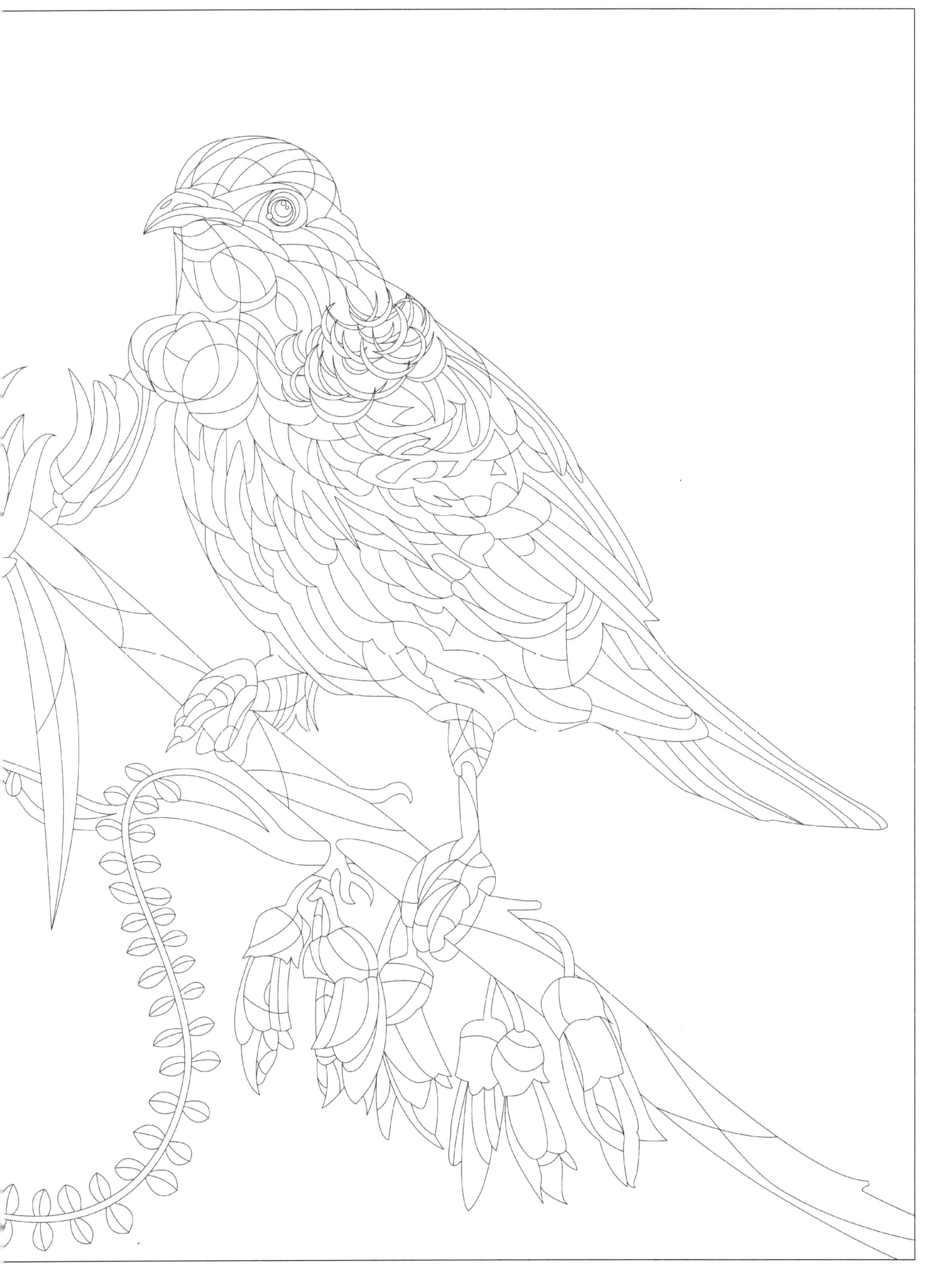

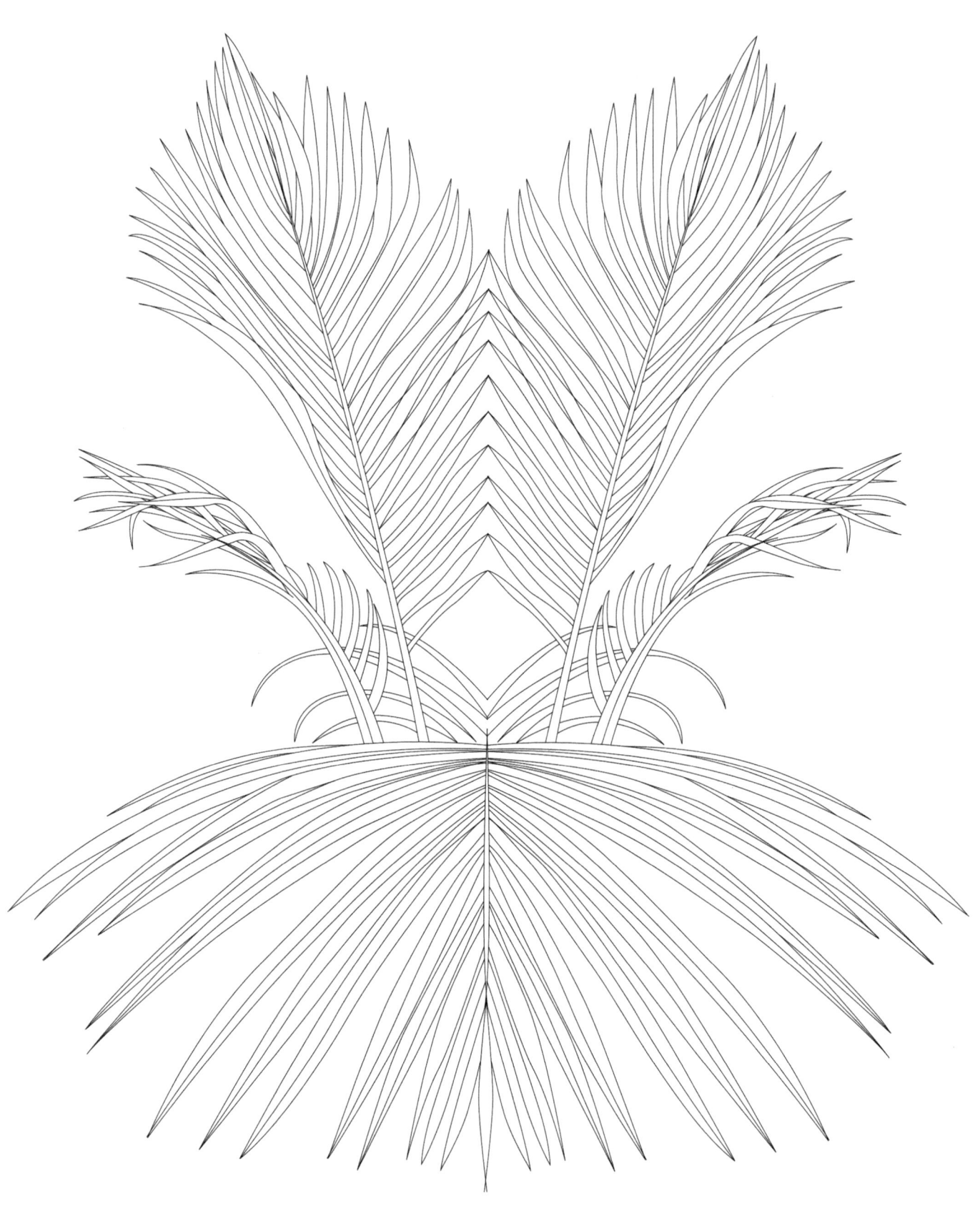

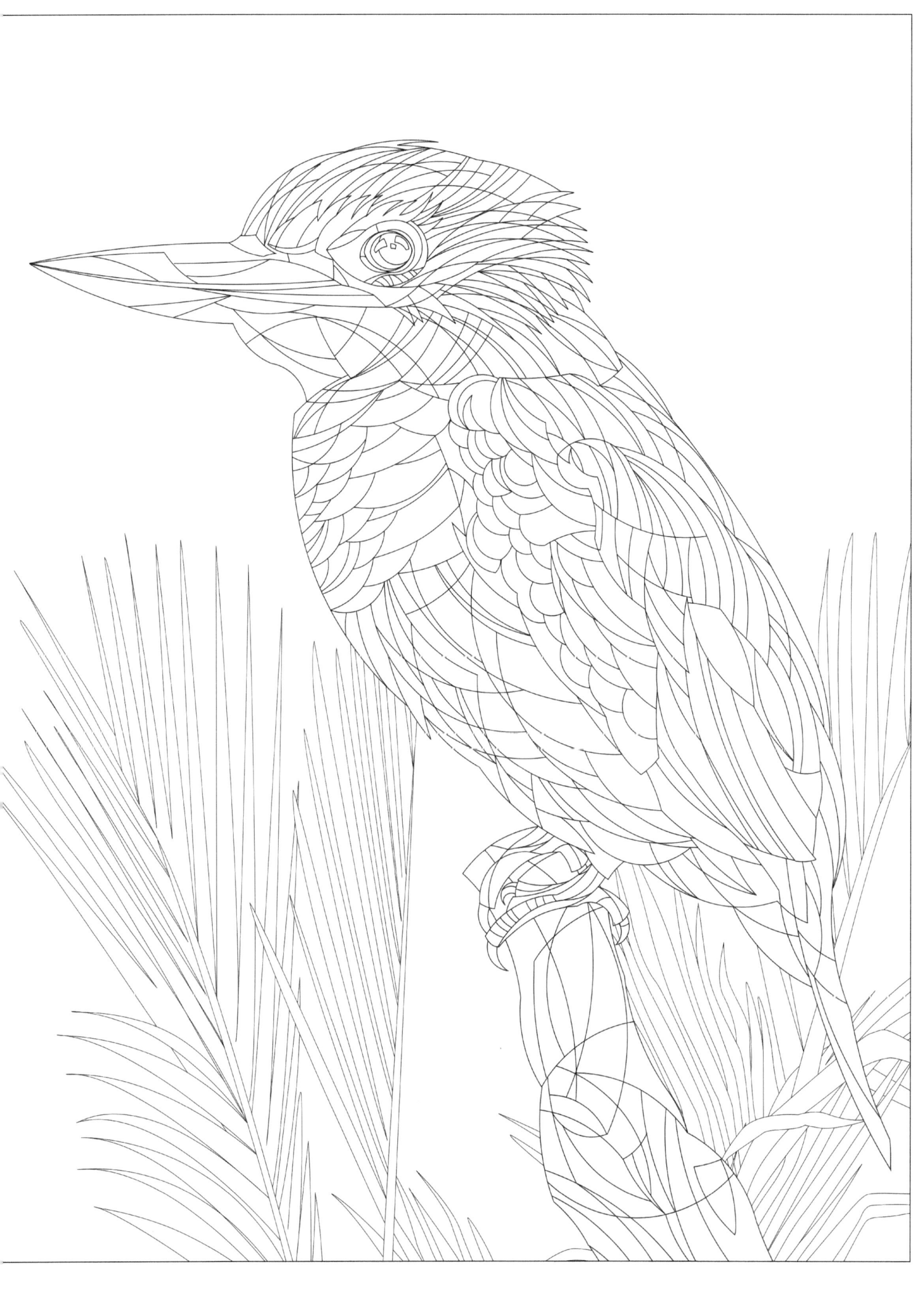

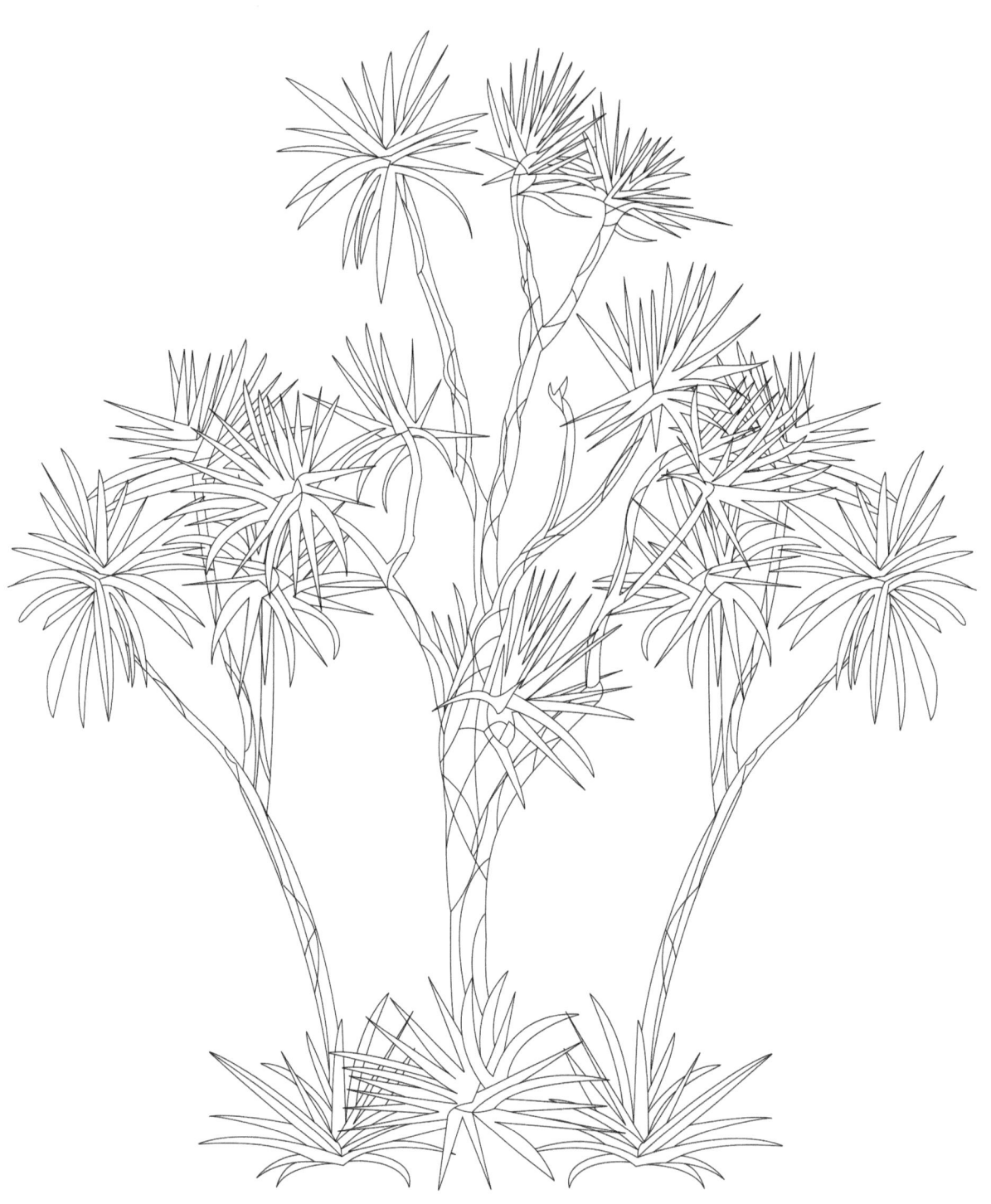

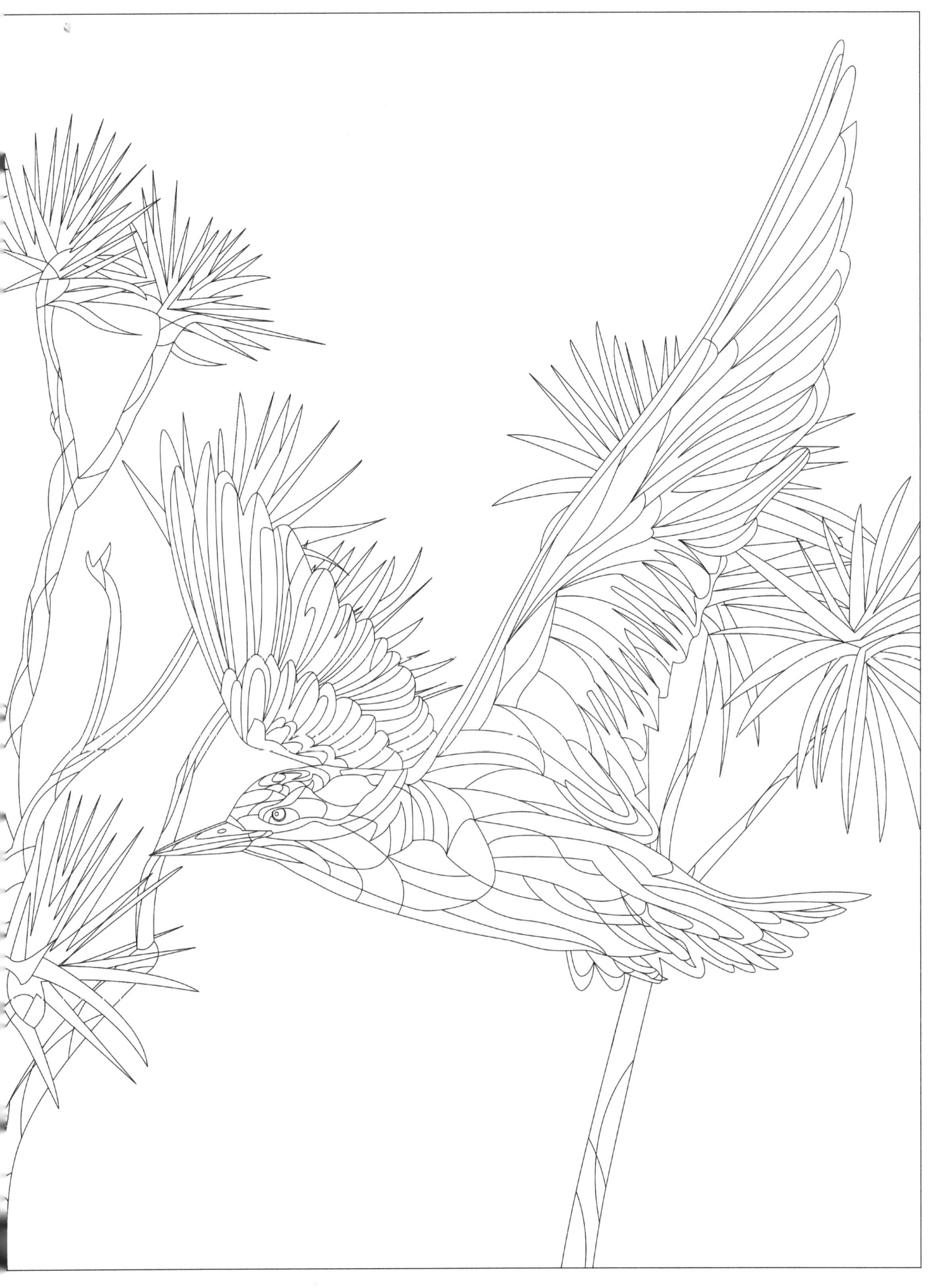

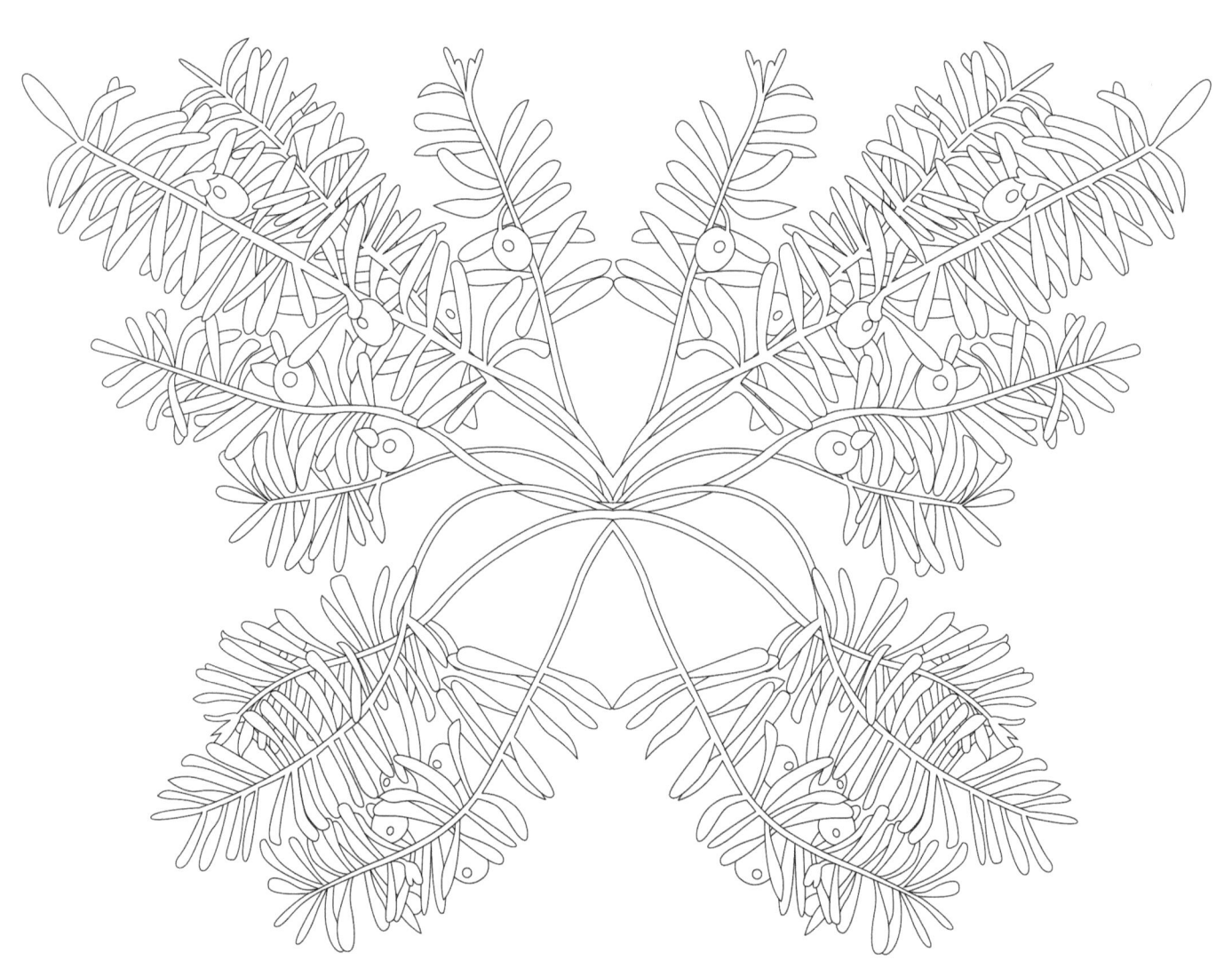

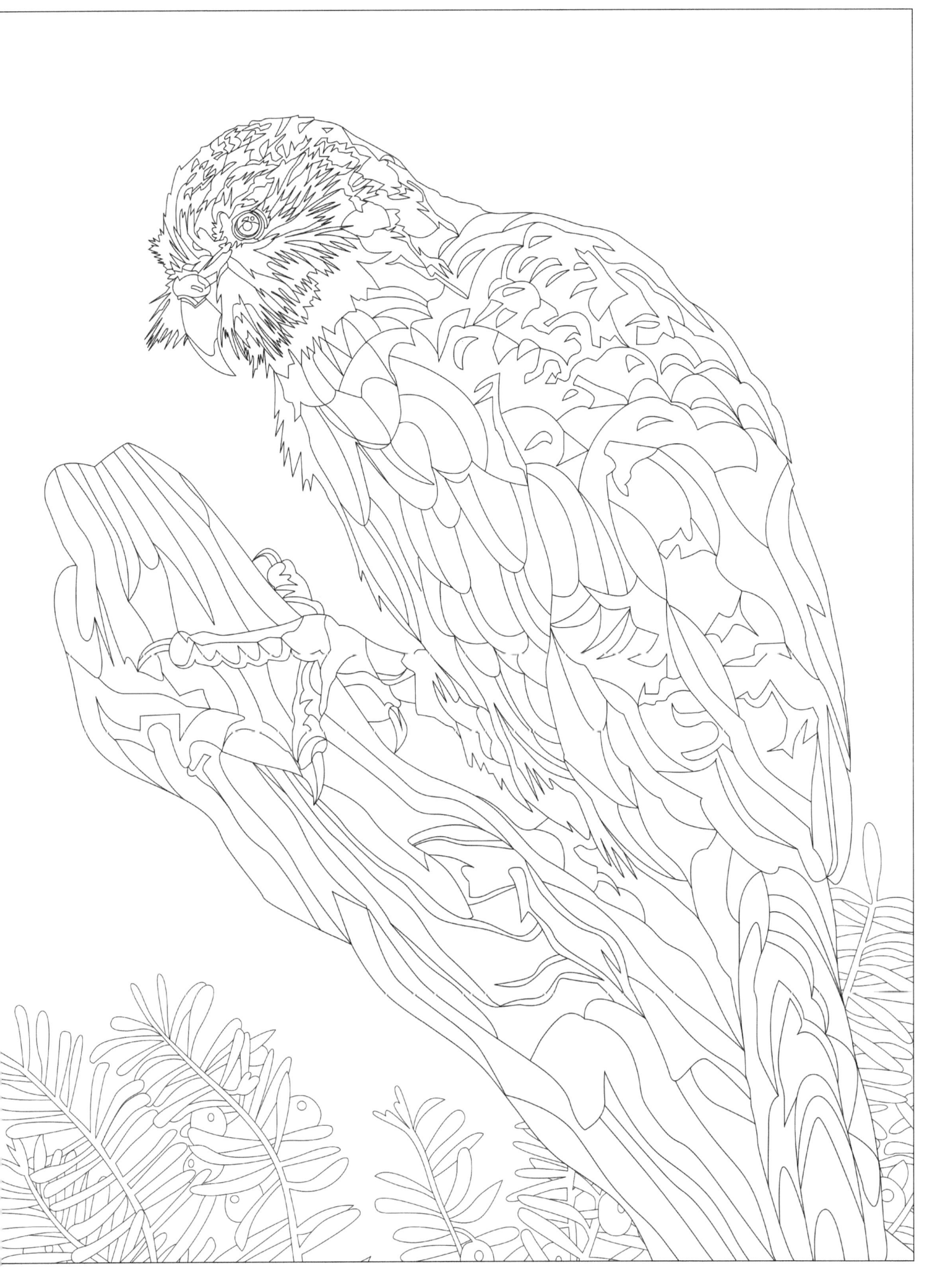

www.ingramcontent.com/pod-product-compliance
Lightning Source LLC
Chambersburg PA
CBHW051105180526

45172CB00002B/785